LICENTIAPOETICA

Poetic License

by

SOCRATEEZ

Enchanted Muze Publishing

Houston

Printed in the United States of America

Licentia Poetica, Poetic License

ISBN: 978-1-930112-04-9

Enchanted Muze Publishing
www.heathenshouse.com

Cover Design and Photography:
Elton McWashington
emc2artwork.com

10 9 8 7 6 5 4 3 2 1

Dedication

This book is dedicated to **anyone** who has
ever touched me: Kathie, Chan, Xavier
my family (immediate & extended)
The Small's & The Thomas'
My family at
Texas Southern University, High Volume Music,
New Power Houston, AF&A Masons and OES's,
and the numerous artist and musicians whose music
has **constantly** inspired me... especially
The Artist Formerly Known As Prince
(thanks Bruh... you don't have a clue :-)

**Stay hard, Stay perky, and
Stay TRU**

Contents

Introduction

People often say they cannot "feel" poetry. They say it is hard to grasp, and often on a level that they are not on. Why so many people feel they cannot write or read poetry is beyond my grasp. If one is to be able to really enjoy poetry, one must first get in touch with one's inner self. Once the inner self has been found, then it is easy to understand what someone else is attempting to say.

This collection of work is easy to read (it is "reader friendly"), simple to grasp, and on a level **anyone** can understand. Although many of the words may be new to you, the message is old. This book, like any collection of poems, addresses one issue: life. Poetry has a way of penetrating one's core consciousness, and allowing the reader to feel what the poet is offering. Given the opportunity, I want to allow you (the reader) to delve into my world. If you can understand the words on the page, you can understand the message I'm relaying. As with any journey, there are no certain paths. There are several roads that may lead you to a particular destination. Poetry is my path. This collection is simply a ten year "map" as to where I've been. In my "short" time I have been able to savor the joy, pain, and all the in betweens in this work.

I do not declare or profess to be the most prolific poet, but I do believe in my work (as anyone should). The pieces on these pages are **my** feelings, **my** thoughts, **my** passions... **My** life. If my life can help someone in their pain, assist someone through their pleasure, or be good reading for a few, my publishing this material is not in vain.

It is my intention to bring out the poet in everyone who reads this book. From a simple thought to a complex composition, the fire of life burns in us all. It would be inhumane to **not** satisfy your soul. It is hard to imagine one experiencing this **dream** we call life, and never being touched by at least one poem. Inception to completion, we **all** have something to say.

POSSUM, POTES, POSSUMUS
I am able, You are able, We are able

In a collection of work I highly recommend entitled *Living, Loving, Learning*, Leo Buscalia says:

Because you are human, you do have magic. Get in touch with it.
When you feel insanity rising, don't push it down. Let it come out.

Everyone is a poet

Licentia Poetica

Poetry is...
The screaming of your
heart
The whispers of your
soul
The tingling of your
mind
Poetry is...
The dancing of your
skin
The severing of your
nerves
The awakening of your
senses
Poetry is...
Mortality and Moribund
Peace and Plagues
Pleasure and Pain
Poetry is...
All that you have
become
and
Everything you dream

LUX

Light

NON SCHOLEA SED VITAE DISCIMUS - SENECA

We learn not for school, but for life

"Happiness comes only when we push our brains and hearts
to the farthest reaches of which we are capable... The
purpose of life
is to matter-to count, to stand for something, to have it
make some
difference that we lived at all" - Leo Buscalia

Trivial Space

Why should I seek
Death like a blind
hunter calling for his prey?
My mission is not completed, nor is
my faith exhausted
So, why am I the lonely one?
I have packed all that my
back will allow, but is it
sufficient?
Is the strain, coupled with the pain,
justified in my vicarious position?
I have crawled in woods serpents would
not dare, yet I find myself
longing for more
More uncharted or more unexplored?
More less daring or more the less bored?
Even Death, with her secluded sights,
presents herself once in a night
Clandestine or clear, the hour draws
near, to find my place in this trivial space

riddles or ridiculous

how can i say that my heart
bleeds, when water runs through my veins?
how can i say i am
sorry, when tomorrow is not the same?
how can i
forgive, when i cannot forget?
how?
is this a trial, or
is this my conviction?
which is worse? do i
apologize for my actions, or do
i accept my acknowledgement?
questions with no resolution
resolutions for unasked questions
unasked questions that have been replied
riddles or ridiculous,
i know not
what is known is the time, and
that is only an approximation
what is sacred? what is pure? what is tried?
the answer to all, is the answer to none
i labor in this prison erected
to me for me
for what purpose?
to what end?
why?

Illusions

All has become an illusion
Looking through stained glass windows,
I see shadows that are vaguely familiar
I seek to find something...
I have searched for so long, that what I find
possesses none of the qualities that I desire
I obtain it and make it what I want,
when it is nothing I need

All has become an illusion
No time for thought now, my
instincts are overriding all
Survival is the key here
But where am I?
Feeling with my hands,
instead of my heart
Seeking my desire still,
but adhering to my duty
Knowing right from wrong,
and stuck somewhere between the two
Although destiny is predetermined,
it can be slightly altered
What is it that keeps me walking
aimlessly through uncharted lands?
I cannot change the past, however,
it is difficult to accept my future
Pleasure is a paradox, and
duty is disturbing
How can a blind man see,
if his eyes are never opened?

If I opened myself a thousand times,
I would still be closed to infinite bliss!
Either way, I am paralyzed to both
pleasure and pain
I have been subjected to survive
with a little of nothing left
The two have not become one here
There is either one or the other
There are no mediums... here
No shades or fractions of gray
Where am I?

I know that there are seven levels to Hell,
however,
I do not recall making it to the first
I am neither beat nor burned
So, where in Hell am I?
Am I in Hell?
My Hell is too horrid
and
My Heaven is too far
All has become an illusion

Proposed Paradise

A single idea is
    born
  Like a spark that
      gives life to a fire
      the idea births a
  thought
Nations are born
Governments crumble
A new life begins
  Aimless wonder is
      no more, once the process
  begins
  Set into motion is a
    notion that cannot be
        prolonged
We seek and die for
  elements that both
    onset and undo
  Found only in an
    idea, we contemplate,
                comprehend,
          and construct
If...
  A word many a men have
    lied upon
If I beget
  Should
Should I beget
  Could
Could I beget
  Would
Would I beget

Didn't
Did not is only a
   bastard bairn
   from what may have been
But these are all
   obliged orphans of
      idea and reason
   From idea and reason
      spawns logic
Logic is that which we
   all desire
      But like all fires,
   it dies all to quickly
What remains is a
   senseless notion of a
   proposed paradise

Truth... In Time

Lend your ears to the truth
Nothing is ever black or white...
   it is only a hazy shade of Grey
Although black pedals and red roses
    fall from the sky
       a strong wind from the south is aching
I sit and listen to the same
   melody over and over again
    as if it were a mermaid's tale
I muse truth and its substance
   and suddenly
     I hear a new song

I've come to the understanding that
   truth is only what a man
     makes it
We shape truth like religion...
   to fit our purpose
    I've stumbled onto a never-ending story
Morality is shaped by religion...
Religion is shaped by man...
Man is shaped by his egocentric
   desires to be satisfied
    By any means necessary
These are the things I believe
   I hold these truths to be self-evident
    not because I've sat for so long

but because truth has a way of making itself
known
So, what then molds and shapes
the world?
Time
Time heals, purifies, and creates
Time wounds, infests, and destroys
Time reveals all mysteries, yet
Time camouflages the known
Time, apathetic in nature, soothes
the aching heart...
yet, She makes ones heart ache
Time, an apparition of her own right and
form, is likened unto Destiny
They exist and observe, but not to
interfere
For she is not an interim, but an
undeniable entity encompassing eternity
I have sought after Time, but she
moves too fast for me
For she is like the tide
they wait for no man

Truth may be what men make it,
but Time shall always be Time

Shapes and Colors

Soft glowing
present showing
always knowing
this is what
rainy mornings
makes me feel
I do not know why
but yesterday
seemingly
kicks in and the
horror is once more
It can not be
subsided only
guided
but where to...
I do not know
Why
Today is only a reminder
but of what...
I do not know
Circles of passion
and squares of grief
Triangles of truth
and lines of reality
Verticals are yours
Horizontals are mine
Is it a paradox,

or a play of perception
Linear understanding
or
curved reality
Realism is relative
and
truth is testimonial
Tetchy, life can be
with no short distances
Only proven paths
Revolutionary
or self-explanatory
When charity is
dressed, it is still
and notable
When charity is
naked, it moves
often unnoticed
This is my reality
I do not know whither
error is human
or
foolish
But with charity,
error is void
I error not as a
result of, but yet
in charity
I am a fool to hold
onto footsteps and
not cherish my feet
nor my path
The sound of sunbeams
brighten my day
I look for error
where none exists
Critically I stare

at charity dressed
in an ideal, and
I wonder why
Black or White
absorbing or reflecting,
I wonder when...
Grey...
Medium...
taking and giving
Taking my end
Giving my inception
I am a medicant,
a moocher
For what,
I do not know
What I do know,
Is that I dread
rainy mornings

Perhaps

Sometimes I hurt,
  and I don't know why
Often times, there is pain,
  but there are no bruises
Consequently, I want to cry,
  but I know not why
Perhaps my past is seeking
  vengeance
Perhaps the present does not like its
  path
Perhaps the future is filled with too much
  fantasy and no reality
    Perhaps
Perhaps there is a forest of trees with no leaves,
  nor roots to call their own
Perhaps there is a castle that sits in the clouds,
  but the gods must have abandoned it
Perhaps rivers cease to flow,
  because tears have watered their paths
Perhaps empty skies are filled with stars,
  and Grey skies were always blue
Perhaps lost loves were never lost, yet
  they are only in hiding
Perhaps broken dreams are mended with hope
         Perhaps

Wishes of a Wiseman

If the desires of a man's
  heart could speak,
    how many sunsets would pass
      before my heart was heard?
I've often tried to make my
  ambitions known, but I am
    likened unto a child quarreling with its
    parents.
Although I conjure up the thoughts,
  the words never fall from my lips.
Though the stage is set,
  the scene has not yet begun.
The time to be heard is now,
  but do I have the courage or faith to act?
It appears to me that mine is
  as a seed falling on stony ground;
    or better, a voice being carried by the
      wind falling on deaf ears.
  I want so much, but receive so little.
  I reject too much, but accept so little.
  I desire too much, and need so little.
If the world were mine,
  would my thirst be quenched?
Only a fool desires the world,
  but a wise one resides in it.
I have learned to let the rain
  fall where it may; I have learned
    to be patient.
Through the turbulent times,
  I have learned to be content.
From my ignorance,
  I have learned to appear wise.
Could it be that I am a fool
  with wise wishes, or wise
    with foolish desires?

Farsighted Faith

Faith and fear is the separation many Christians can not face. There is a fine line between the two, and too often we **fall** on the wrong side of the dividing line. What does it mean to "step out on faith"? How do I hide, or rather suppress, my inhibitions of my fear? Why do I struggle with my ability to succeed, fearing the failure I may face? These three questions haunt Christians, causing our downfall. If one can look beyond the fear of failure, then it is my belief that farsighted faith flabbergast the Christian to a large level of immediate success.

A Simple Thought

Struggling to reach my peak, I am afraid of what lies beyond the summit. Am I weak? Am I frightened? Am I capable of reaching the unthinkable? Though my arms cannot lift much, they can support my dreams. Although I am not certain about tomorrow, I know if I do not try, I will fail for sure. If I allow others to control my thoughts, I will never know what to think for myself. No goal is unthinkable, because it took a thought to label it unthinkable. All it takes is a **thought**, followed by a **will** or **desire**, and finished with an **action**. Where will my desire take me? What action will follow my will? I pray that it is the right one!

Glimpse At Greatness

People tend to ask me why do I do many of the odd
things I do. My answer usually is, because I like to be
unique. I like to keep qualities that differ greatly from the
norm. To me, uniqueness is the spice of life. It gives people
choices and allows room for change. In examining myself
or understanding my perception of me, I see myself
as an educator of God's people chosen to give them
choices.
The three most important influential areas this occurs in
is among my friends, at school, and at the church.

Among my friends, I am a role model for those
who look to the young for guidance. My friends feel I
can actually be admired because of the title I hold. Even
among them, I give them choices in
my uniqueness.

At school, I try to be unique in my application in
all I do. I do everything, not in correspondence to what
the world wants, but according to how I feel they should
be done.

At church, everything I do is distinct. I think
being a leader in the Christian church, I must be more
appealing than the next guy; give the people more than
just the usual. So, therefore, I am as peculiar as I can be.

If you can accept me, fine. If you cannot
accept me, fine. But I will continue to be me and
unique as possible.

My perception of me is great.

Anticipation

The feeling of your
mind rushing like
the wind
The touch of your
body being pricked by
ten thousand needles
The taste of your
sweetest victory knowing
defeat is not far away
The sight of your
honor being abused
to gain attention
The smell of your
soul marching closer
to Death
Can you hear it?
Is any of this familiar?
Has your world begun to crumble?
Although life leaks from you with
Despair, Courage whispers in your ear
I wonder...
Are those sweet words?
Touch me, tease me, ease my
pain, release me from these shackles that keep me
sane

Truth's Cloak

This is not the end
  nor is this the beginning
This is the medium you have
    left me
  Staying right is not one of my
    best points
      but it is not my worst
I could lie and say I am not
    affected
      but that is only a fabrication of
      the truth
  In all reality, truth is like a
    fine fabric
  On the surface
      the beauty is magnificent
But a closer look
      displays the detail
        Once put together
          it is a fine garment to adorn one
        Be ye careful as to not pull the
            loose strings
      It is only magnificent, if you let it be
You need not worry about the
          straggling string
    It harms no one
      but it may unravel
        leaving the master naked
Force is a fine means to
    create an end
  This appears premature...
      rushing that which was bound
        to be

Frigid and bare
        I know I am not alone
For the cloak of truth has
        resolved for me many times
        leaving me naked
                        plain
                        and frigid
        I know I am not alone
        But this,
                child,
                        is the legacy I leave to you
Gird yourself in truth's cloak
        For it may appear worn and olden
        But golden is its beauty
                and delicate is its detail
        For it will keep you clothed
                This is all I know
                        I know I am not alone

Displacement

Last night,
  I cried for the first
time in a thousand tears
  I thought of things you
promised, and I cried
  I thought of things I
promised, and I cried
  I thought of things We
promised, and I died
  I drowned in an empty
oasis filled with lies
    Like wishes that have
        fallen like
    stars from the sky,
  I fell hard
        Staggering to reach the
lighthouse, Time tells me
  I am early
    As I patiently wait for
  the other guests, I
entertain Pain and Grief
I wonder...
    Who gets the
    first dance?
After idle conversation and
  thoughtless concentration,
    Love retrieves me
She tells me I have no
    place among the
    Sisters of Sorrow
    so we leave
I awake next to the

oasis, only to find
that Love made her
way to you as well
Can we continue on our
journey, or do you
wish to take another
bath?

Bed of Thorns

So many nights, I've laid
  my head on pillows of
    confusion
Lost, were my thoughts
   to untimely trials
No one could adopt my
    pain, but I'd like to
  share it
My bed, prickly to the touch,
  is made of thorns
      Every time I twist and turn
    from dreams undreamed, I'm
  pierced in the side for my
transgressions
  Wounded for my
    iniquity, I search for some
      solitary province that deems me a
   slave
  Noticing that I survive not
from my own strength, but from the strength of
  others, I seek to save myself
For the thorns have choked
  the roses, causing them to
    wither and die
These deeds cannot go unpunished,
  nor can they be ignored
I have to right the
   wrongs...
I have to remake
  my bed, so that I may
    lie in it again
For thorns have grown like

wildflowers, now it is time to
tend to my chores
      I must cut the thorns, and let
        the roses grow once more
      I must allow time for healing,
        and nourish the buds
      I must tend to my Eden,
        and rid it of weeds
      I must refine my room,
        and free it from ignorance
      I must, and I shall, get my
        house in array and advance with
          my life

Cry For Help

People tend to believe they can
think for me
They may as well say that,
since they claim they
know how i feel
How in the hell do you
know how i feel?
How can you know what i
feel, unless you know me
and all that i've been
through
all that i've seen
all that i've felt
You don't know me, and i
know not of you
You don't know what i've
seen, what i've been
through, and damn sure don't know
how i've felt
So, don't say you know how i
feel, just lend me your
support
Give me a brace
to endure what i
must
Can you feel my heart?
Can you feel my mind?
Can you feel my soul?
Don't lie and say you
feel my pain, because
you don't
Don't fabricate and say you

ache for my pleasure, because
you won't
Just give me a brace
to endure what i
must
Just lend me your
support

Can I Dream?

Last night, I had a dream
  Not just any ordinary dream,
  but a very extraordinary dream
    A dream that fulfilled the dreams of others,
    was found in the dream I had last night
    The dream I had last night was one that
    I shall never forget
    I had a dream inwhich I was actually
    Somebody
    I was actually someone with
      Respect   Someone to be
      Admired
    For in my dream I was not
        just someone, but I was someone
      Special
    I was a special someone who **all**
    children wanted to be
But what then is the difference
between the dream and who I am
now you may ask?
Nothing! Absolutely nothing
There is nothing different, I was
Me... nothing more, nothing less
But it was just a dream,
Right? It was all just a
dream
Could I really be
admired,
respected, or have some
authority?
In my dream, I could do all things
    But someone told me I could do

30

nothing... someone told me that I would
never amount to anything
Someone told me that I could not
succeed in society, and have
authority,
admiration, or
respect

But allow me this dream,
for I have dreamed all night
I have dreamed all night for every
night of my life
So, let this dream be **mine**,
for a dream is all
I have

A Tale To Tell

As the color of my hair fades
   and the vivid memories of yesteryear die,
I wonder how the rest of my days
   will be spent and often wonder why.
I look for my friends,
   but it seems they have passed.
I wish to speak of days gone by,
   but it seems they, too, do not last.
I seek my family,
   for I wish to tell them a tale.
I had hoped they would hear me out,
   but they have no time for an old man.
I pray to the angels,
   for they have always answered my call.
I fear they have forsaken me.
There must be a heavenly gathering going on.
I have yelled out into the night,
"Hear me, hear me, he who has ears"
   but too often the moon does not shine,
     and the wind blows cold.
I have been forced to tell Nature,
   but even her children ignore me.
   When I try to speak to the wind,
     it blows on toward the world's corners.
   When I attempt to speak to the trees,
     my message falls from their leaves.
   When I plead with the river to listen to me,
     it only rolls onward to speak to the sea!

What shall I do, oh my Lord, What shall I do?
   I am tired, and the voices of four million
     siblings speak to me.
What shall I do? For I have spent countless nights

tossing and turning, running from the
demon within.
When I lay my head on my pillow,
   I long to journey to the golden streets of Heaven.
      For I am told the gates are made of pearls,
         and the rivers flow with diamonds.
      They tell me there will be no more
         crying, and the days of dying will be
            done.
      I have heard people speak of the
         silver city, and I have tried to
            envision it.
But when I lay my head on my pillow,
   I dream of pain, not pleasure;
            sacrifice, not serenity;
            persecution, not peace.
      When I dream, I see ships and chains;
                        deceit and destruction;
                        murder and mayhem.
               I see faces like mine, young and old;
               I see the stories of many that have never
                  been told.
               I see a young prince who will never be
                  King.
               I see a young princess who has been
                  raped
                  of her royalty.
      When I dream, I often think of names
         I have never known;
            names of a Nation within a nation, that was
               castrated in order to not produce a
                  greater Nation.

I hear names that may have very well
be my own name, but I know not
which one.
I hear names that make the sun rise
and
I hear names that make the earth
shake!
I hear names that the gods have
given my people,
and
I hear names that God has known for
ages.
I hear names of those that have either
settled with the sand,
been buried at sea, or
have been beaten and hung from
trees.
How can I be expected to sleep,
when the voices from the past wake the
sleeping demon within?
How can I think of Heaven, when my
siblings have been subjected to Hell?
How can I stay silent, when they
my people, have a story to tell?
As the color of my hair fades
and vivid memories die,
I think of how the rest of my days
will be spent never asking why.
You seek to know my story, or better still
ask me what shall I do?
I shall tell my story to all I can,
my story: My Nation Before 1492

AMORE
Love

SUMMON BONUM
The greatest good, and source of all other benefits

"I think one of the greatest destructive elements in relationships and intimacy is our inability to relate what we're feeling now"

- Leo Buscalia

A Love Melody

There is a smile on my face.
For some reason, I feel life.
I feel what I haven't felt
For a while. I can hear a
Love melody like no other.
The song is sung by unknown
Artist, yet her voice makes me
Quiver. Though I cannot see her,
I know she is there. She sits in a
Dark room waiting to be known.
But I, I cannot see her. All
I can do is hear her sensual
Voice.

Is that so bad? With only
The ability to hear her, I know I
Want her. In her song she
Seduces me. She takes me to that
Utopia I've been searching for
When she speaks. But if I could
Only see her. If I could only get a
Glimpse of her, then maybe I could
Appreciate her evermore. Maybe, if I could
See, I could discover what light
Shines behind the darkness.
Maybe I should open my eyes.

Born Again

Grey skies that are no longer Grey,
but Black...
Two moons set in the east,
while yet another lingers
in the air above...
Wishes that have
fallen like
stars from the sky...

To live without Love,
or love with need...
pricked my heart,
and made my soul bleed
Walking aimlessly,
never finding my heart's desire

Finding you,
was by fortune
Loving you,
is by grace

Beauty balanced only by Heaven
You have rained drops
of love on this dying
heart of mine

The sun does not
rise without your smile,
nor does the night
fall without your touch
Now that I have found you,
Heaven does not seem so far away
Now that I have you,
I know Heaven is where I have always belonged
Without you,
I am extinct
With you,
I'm born again

Sparkle

Have you seen her?
If you have seen her,
then you would know why I ask

When she speaks,
Angels are quick to listen
The way she delivers
is enough to mesmerize
the furies
When she moves,
Heaven stops to watch
The way she walks
is enough to captivate
any bystander in his innocence
When she examines,
she more than satisfies her viewer
The way she looks
traps even the widow in black

How can I not be affected,
when she speaks to more than my heart?
How can I not be affected,
when she passes by more than my mind?
How can I not be affected,
when she looks at more than my soul?

I pray she sees more than
an hour of pleasure...
a month of ecstasy...
I pray she sees a
lifetime of love

I have dreamed of her for so long,
it hardly seems real
Her essence entraps me
like an animal in the wild
I've lurked in the
shadows of time,
waiting to seize her

Soft and gentle
Pleasant and kind
Elegant and beautiful
Light as the morning's rise
and
dark as the sun's set

She lights up the night
with her smile
and
blesses the day
with her touch

It's no wonder why she sparkles!

You Are

As I lay in my bed,
  I can't help but stare at
Your picture.
  Although it is a photograph of
Us,
I see no me; I only see
  You and all the beauty you
  Possess.
You are an aesthetic experience
  In its truest form,
  As you are beauty defined.
    The two gems you call eyes are as
    Pure as the Caribbean waters; yet,
  They are as dark and mysterious as
The heavens above.
  With your refined eyes,
  You look right through me to see my
Soul.
  My soul can do nothing but yield,
As your seductive, sensual words
  Befall your gracious lips.
  The sound of your voice caresses
Me and makes me feel new.
  Your hair lies on your head
    Like the fresh morning dew.
  Your smile is sunshine that
    Beams into the hearts of
  Many.
  You are an Egyptian Queen,
    And I am to hold you in the
    Highest esteem.
  You are to be seen and admired

By all,
But forsaken by none.
You are truly God's Gift to man;
God's gift to this man.
So, without adding any other
Words, because you are
Everything beauty
Wants to be;
You are.

Communion

Is there ever a
  day, when the sun ceases and
  the rain falls?
Is there a
  moment, when time stands still and
  forever continues?
Is there ever a
  chance, that tomorrow will be there and
  today is only a prelude?
What can be said about the
    aimless wanderer who cannot find his way?
What can be known about the
    song composed during the witching hour?
Where is the joy in a dead man's passage?
If I can pry for a moment, let me share my
  grief
    I know you are young
    I know you are naive
    I know you are scared
      Take my hand
        Close your eyes
          Open your heart
    Is Love so blind,
    She cannot feel my pain?
    Is Despair so nonchalant,
    She does not care to intervene?
    Is Pride so powerful,
    He does not assist the powerless?
  I pray I am not the
prize of their joust
  I hope that I am not the
field of their battle

I fear my faith is not as
strong as my desire
        Signs and symbols have I none
        I only have a token of myself
        A small hexagram is my talent
    non compos mentis
        I am afflicted with irrationality
        and mental instability
    Can my condition be improved?
    With your assistance, I feel light may shine
        An emphatic wind wisps in my ear
            reminding me of the beauty bestowed in you
        Irrational,
            I am not sure
        Unstable,
            Maybe
        Insane,
            Definitely!
Every moment with you makes me agrestial
    Accept
    Adopt
        and enfold my soul
Spiral is the motion and
    keen is the notion that
        You are my direction
        Find me
        for **Communion**

The Rose, The Journey

A single rose rises amid a
field of thorns
Gasping for air
Hoping to live
Seeking to love
A broken ring lies on the stem and
A single stone sits on the other
The ring is made of lead and
the stone, a lapis philosophorum
a philosopher's stone
This emergence comes as no surprise
For I have longed to discover this beauty
Never let it be said I was never the journeyman
Never let it be said that I was never in on the hunt
To the east of the thorn field,
lies three colorful roses
St. John's three
light
love
life
Is this a figment of my imagination,
Or is this a symbol of things to come?
I cannot express to you the path I am to take
I can only find you there, in the middle of the field
For it is you,
my rose,
that lies in the midst of thorns
It is not only my duty,
but my honor
that makes me
march on
I am told that a combination of the three jewels

found will magically make gold
How good and pleasant it would be,
to find you next to me
adorned with
that
which many search for
You are my rose,
You are my jewel,
You are my journey

Cupid

Is it my nature
to be read like a page in
Destiny's scroll?
Though words appear on the
script, they change with every passing
second
My crest is as the moon,
which as fate would have it,
never shining as bright as the
sun
The light I give is both
misleading and manipulative
I can lead you through a
journey, but I cannot take you to its
inception
My expression may
begird you, but I cannot let you
loose
Odd... numerals, counts, ticks
I belong to no triad
I am me
There is no one else
How can I make you see
that which cannot be seen
Though you measure me,
I still elude you
Once we begin,
there is no return
Retreat is not an option
Surrender, the only relic that remains
Words, white flags, and blood stained cloths
How do you give in?

Words would be preferred
White flags seem so flagrant
Blood stains are
often cloudy
Begging is always good
Will I ever cease?
That is too easy
Why not torture you more?
I know I can, and
I think I will
Sweet victory
Can you taste defeat?
I've won and you have lost
Don't hate me, embrace me
You knew I was coming
And all the preparations you have made
were useless
My light still caught you
Don't lose your way
For I am not a guide,
I am merely a
Gorge

Summer Solstice

Summer winds and winter rains
  blow calmly in my mind...
The rain beats the pain
  of a love gone bad
    from my aching heart
I am haunted by a
  melody, but I do not know why
I look from a
  distance
I see the cloud's tears
With mixed emotions,
  the sky screams in torment
I feel his anguish
Through the window's pain,
I see I am not alone
The ease of the symphony
  that plays in my mind
    puts my soul to rest...
I am never too far
  from the song, but I have
    not heard its tune in four moons
If I never see you,
  will you love me?
If I never feel you,
  will you love me?
If I never taste you,
  will you love me?
Since what should not be
  is, is it too late
    to say yes?

Never End

The morning dew is
falling quietly,
putting the grass to rest
The sun begins to rise,
breaking the night
in two
i await this glory,
for i know there is nothing more
majestic, nothing more
royal, nothing more
beautiful
i have dreamed of this day
many nights

i stand in the middle of a
field, facing the east
facing the sun
The northern wind offers me
protection
The western wind surrenders
my direction
The southern wind prohibits
my own insurrection

A gypsy told me things
regarding the dream
i have been dreaming

She said
my love is like the sun
The sun, which is the essence of all life
The sun, which defines beginnings
The sun, which sets all endings
my sun has begun to rise,
and thus my heart
my day is set
my life has an origin,
but like the sun,
it shall set
What am i to do?
Where am i to turn?
Who then shall i turn to?

One has come my way
who is like the wind
gentle... soft... kind... She
comes from the
north... west... south... She
seeks to
protect... direct... liberate... Me
Her love is the elixir of life itself
Pure is her heart, and
open is her soul
She is the ending to this beginning
i have begun
Without her, the dream can
never end

Searching For Love

There is an island, far away,
 That man searches for;
  It is a paradise, a haven,
   A field of dreams that all
    Search for.
     In this utopia, the grass is green
      Beyond imagination. The trees there
     Are gloriously adorned with green
     Foliage. The fragrance of the flowers
 Is so entrapping, it carries the large
Burdens off of your heavy heart.
 The hills all tend to roll to
  Eternity, and there is always
   A rainbow to remind you of
    Your beautiful day.
     I at one time inhabited this
     Garden of Eden, but I have
    Been cursed with a curse.
   I've been cast out, and it seems
  I am to never return.
What was once paradise,
 Is now a paradise lost.
  What men have searched and
   Died for,
    I have found.
     What most crave and lust for,
     I have tasted.
    What many have only dreamed,
   I have lived; Now I wish I
  Were like them: For it is better
To have never loved at all,
 Than to have lost a love!

54

See, when you spend your life searching
  For a certain fountain,
    Nothing can quench your thirst but
    That well.
    And even if you do not understand,
    Time shall reveal all mysteries.
  Nothing beneath the sun has
Permanence, but one thing is
Certain: everything must and will
Change.
  In between all our lives
    Expectations, we seek
    What was, what is, and
      What shall be. And I guess we
      Wonder along the highways of our lives
      Wishing, hoping, dreaming for all
    We seek.
  But if you never know what you want,
You will never know what you are
  Looking for.

No Questions

someone asked me the other day,
how could i let you go?
i looked deeply into their eyes,
and said it was all to easy.
when someone who has dreamed the
same dreams you have no longer
dreams of you, then you understand
dreams don't last forever.
it becomes that much easier to let them go.
Despair once told me that
when your best efforts
fall short of the mark...
when tears no longer fall from your
eyes, but are instead replaced with sorrow...
when dreams slowly fade, and
nightmares begin...
... then, it is time to move on.
so, i say to you, keep walking and never, ever
turn back.
there is nothing left here for you,
except empty aspirations and a
bag full of shattered dreams.
sorrow filled eyes await your
intrusion, and an aching heart
is cursed by you.
but as for how i feel, i have
No Questions.

Belonging

Looking beyond the realm of contentions
and conspiracies into a cafe'
of overheated souls with
bound aspirations as
their inspiration,
is it any wonder
I am confused?

What was once joyful, is now pained
What was once lost, is now gained
What was once clear, is now stained

Is it any wonder
I am confused?
You...
you proclaimed to love me,
but all you bring is rain
Love may sting the heart,
but it does not cut it to its core
Why can't we just be happy?
Why can't we just be right?
Why can't we just be in love?
How can you abandon that
which you love,
unless you never
loved at all
I feel like a cheap infatuation,

living in the shadows of your fascination

Love cannot be built in a day,
but it can be destroyed in a second
I hate you for making me think of you,
when I know you are not thinking of me
I hate you making me want you,
even after you are gone
I hate you for making me need you,
although you do not feel the same
I hate you for making me wait for you,
because you keep me on hold

That, seemingly is the hardest part
to overcome...
the time spent waiting on the love
you sent out
to return
I don't want to wait in vain,
hoping for things you do not
want to work for

Confirm my fears or
grant my fantasies, but
tell me something

If you want me
half as much as I need you,
for loves sake,
believe in me
like I belong to you

A Message of Love

(Dedicated to Monica Odom)

As you grace the world with your presence,
   you delight my heart with your warmth
Your smile brings joy to all our hearts
For as the sun shines on your head,
   the fairies dance at your feet
No simple words could describe you
You've presaged delight into the minds of many,
   and raptured the souls of all you adore
You are a jewel that has no value known to man
Priceless, that's what you are   Priceless
For in the time of trouble, I knew I
   could depend on you
When life became a bore to the point of
   being unbearable, your smile
      fulfilled my heart
You've been more than a confidant,
   a patron, or a friend   When I needed
      you the most; when I needed someone,
      you were there   Thanks to
      God, you've been blessed to be there
   one more year; and I thank Him
   for sending you our way
   We loved, we shared, and we complained
But the love remains, and that's
   all that matters
So, this ode goes out to my
Cousin, my sister, my friend

59

What I See

More than anything said or unsaid,
that hurt the most
It was like taking a sword and
slicing my heart in fours
Inevitably, I must do at least
one thing right in my life
I was late at
my birth,
I made a birth
to early, and
I cannot see the
light of day
Blind and bewildered
I am
Sightful and sincere
She is
For I feel as though I've done
some good, but I have not
done anything right
I have won achievements
(good)
I have won medals
(good)
I have won people
(good)
But I have not done any
one thing right
And if I never see tomorrow,
I would have finally done some
one thing right
Maybe she can see that

You

A Song for Kathie

No one ever said that
the road of love would be
smooth.
Many times, you will come across
obstacles that may make you
stumble and fall
No one ever said that
the road of love would be
straight.

Often times, you will have to turn
a corner, or you may even
come to a crossroads
No one ever stated that
the road of love would always be
filled with joy.
You may walk in the dark
for days, until you
see the sun
And certainly,
No one ever said that
the road of love would not be
lonely.
Seemingly, you may walk
alone, until you discover the
Beauty in a Beast who walks
beside you
Darling, I know I have made the road
rocky, thrown some curves in it, and
probably made you feel as though
you walked alone.
But the last thing I want to do, is

lose your love.
If you would only grab the beasts' hand
who walks beside you, you may
discover the beauty that lies
within.
I dare you to explore all that I have to
offer.
I dare you to examine the taste of life I
set before you.
I challenge you to be a part of everything I
am.
With you, I can
fulfill my destiny...
to create.
Two bodies, but
one mind;
Two hearts, yet
one soul;
Two candles which ignite
one flame that will burn
for eternity.

Can I Kiss You?

Your eyes are too beautiful
To look upon me

Your ears are too innocent
To hear my plea

Your mind is too delicate
To even think of me

Your heart is so loving,
It should never be near me

Your soul is too pure
To experience my rapture

You are too perfect for me
To disrupt your world
Your skin is so soft,
It's as Japanese silk

But your eyes, beautiful as they are,
Shine right through me like sunrays on a
Clear day

Your hair flows
Like the awesome waters of
The great Nile River

You are too perfect for me
To disrupt your world
Me? I'm nothing. I'm no one...
My hair does not flow,
And my eyes do not shine

I do not deserve this opportunity
To even be this close to you
You are too graceful,
Me, I am too grateful
But taking advantage of the opportunity given,

Can I kiss you?
I mean,
May I embrace you
And intrude on your privacy?
Do you mind if I steal a kiss
Like a thief?
Let me creep into your garden
And take a taste of Heaven.
Nothing long, just long enough
To appease my passion...
Would you get vexed if I said
I need you?
Or, would you need me just the same?
Can I kiss you?
A kiss can say so much,
And all I dream to do is express
My need for a seraph
All I want to do is express
My passion for a precious jewel
All I want to do is take a
Wild flower, and treat her like a
Lily in the middle of a field
For as the sun shines,
It illuminates for you
Now, may I kiss you?
May I intrude on your privacy?

All At Once

I thought that I was
incapable of loving again
After being hurt so many times,
it became routine to expect the
worst
I felt as if I had suddenly
stepped into the third dimension,
and I was awaiting the fourth
The love that felt like a
thousand arms caressing my soul,
suddenly became
tiny sharpened edges that were
piercing my heart
I felt as though I would never
love again, nor did I have the
desire to do so
But I was told by a Wiseman that
if ever you need a love,
one will find its way to you
When you are doubtful and in
despair, Love will pick you up
and make you sure
Every since I met you,
my soul has been soothed
of the prior pains
I am sure that Love has made her
way to my heart
Many times, I may never
express the way I feel,
but rest assured
that I do love you
If you never hear the words

fall from my lips,
I am more than thankful for
your presence in my life
You may never know what
impact you have had on my life
Mere words cannot honestly describe
the degree of which I
care for you
But if I must put into words
how I feel, I can only say it feels like
something kind of
wonderful
Like two elements that come together and
explode, we too make
something kind of
wonderful
If God is truly the only
one who knows the hearts of men,
then it is only God who knows
just how much you
make my heart sing
No longer does my heart sing sad
songs, but it rejoices in knowing that
you are near
There is a new light shed on my life,
and I pray that it stays shining
for all to see

I Must Be Dreaming

My days are filled with
tears cried by a mad man
My nights are congested by
rituals of loneliness performed
by Despair
I've been looking through a
dark glass to see a clear world
Visions of gleam and echoes of cheer
haunt my mind like a somber
setting for a funeral
My desires have been illusions,
and my life has been misguided
If dreams solely soar on the
wings of imagination, then my
wounded wings will never fly
for long
I've bruised myself on
broken dreams left behind by those
who had no heart
But I've learned that
broken dreams and empty promises
don't make for much
I know that the only reality,
is the reality of Me
And that
is enough to keep me
more than occupied

For so long, I thought that this
was fantasy, not reality
But, I know me well enough to
know that this reality is capable of

turning heads
This reality is enough to
mold minds, and
shape worlds
This reality is enough to
make dreams come true,
but not without the
you

You have to understand, it takes
two to enjoy a dream by one
With the one and the one
equaling one,
then the two would never
be separate, but
be the same

I'm tired of ailing hearts
and soft spirits
I must be stronger than I
have been in the past
I must be as strong as I
can be, not allowing anything to
break my concentration
For I have a goal,
with a prize
My goal seems to be farthest away
when I'm the closest to it
It's like being trapped in a
labyrinth with no outlet
No matter how I feel I've won,
I've actually lost

No more
I shall play the childish games
no more
For it is time to set sail
for the land of opportunity, and
discover what riches lay in wait
for me

Have I been entertaining dreams
with welcome words of solitude,
or have I been dressed in the
morning dew feeling the sunshine
on my heart?

scattered ashes

every night i try to cry myself to sleep
      i know within my heart,
          this is fantasy trying to see reality
             it is as if i cry invisible tears to
                ease my pain
the reason for my tears
  lies in a realm where i no longer
 exist
a heart i once owned has stopped
 calling me Master
            not that it was a
 slave, but the heart was mine; it
belonged to me
  now the heart i had is hurt, and so am i
  even as i try my best for the maiden
  to notice me,
  she turns and walks away
my best never seems good enough
   what am i to do then? i can do nothing
  for in many ways, i am like a
  mighty Zulu warrior; in other ways,
  i am like a homeless child
   for i am brave, yet i am afraid
   for i am strong, yet i am so weak
   for i am safe, yet i live in fear
maybe i'll just drown in my

River of Tears
then, hopefully, i could live
life like a lonesome dove
my life is becoming as
broken glass: damn near impossible to
put back together
but if i take it slow, it just may
happen
there may be some cuts, but
wounds do heal (in time)
broken glass and shattered dreams thrown
into an invisible river of tears,
is the highlight of my day

Deja Vu

How do you know when to
let go?

Is it when you are no longer
satisfied with what you have?
Is it when you seek for something
somewhere else?

Maybe...

Is it when you cease to look for
answers when you are filled with questions?

Why can't life last forever?
Why can't pleasure be pleasing permanently?
Why can't love last forever?

So many why's, and
not enough why not's
So many tears, and
not enough shoulders
So many pains, and
not enough gauze

Laying in my bed,
I listen to the rain drops on my window
I have no cover, and
it is cold
I am shivering, and
I am scared

Do the answers ever
come?
Does the dawn ever
break?
Does the rain ever
cease?

The lightning is
flashing,
reminding me of
things
I wish to forget
The rain beats
strong,
reminding me my
eyes
have made mistakes
The wind blows
cold,
reminding me my
protection
is weaker than I thought
Deja Vu?
I know I've been
here before
Too many damn
storms
in one night

Am I to blame for all of this...

This apparition from Hell?
I don't recall praying for rain...
If I did, I know I've prayed for it to stop
Am I holding onto something...
Something that keeps the clouds over my head?
Knew I should have buried that brindled calf
(blood still on my hands)

Whether I place it on the
    side of the road,
    bury it, or simply
        forget it,
how do I know when to
    let go?

An Aching Heart

One hundred and twenty two beats per minute,
Yet, my heart is in much grief
Though the eyes can see the naked body,
They cannot see the burning heart
The Pain,
The Grief,
The Agony is so much so,
That the poor heart can hardly endure
Its grief makes the whole body weak
The Legs cannot walk
in the hearts direction
The Feet cannot stand
on the same ground
The Arms cannot lift
the burdens of the heart
The Hands cannot feel
the hurt the heart bears,
Nor can the Mind imagine
what lingers in the heart
The Heart is all alone in
Its quest to find happiness
For as the Heart allots life,
It yields for Death
An aspirin can sustain the mind,
but what can mend an aching heart?

Come Back To Me

I feel like a helpless
child, imitating a lost
soul
My words are muffled, and
my thoughts are confused
Minute by minute, my mind
wonders to Neverland leaving
a trace of tears behind
If I could cry,
I would be treading in
my tears...
wading in the water...
or drowning in my sorrow
All of this is so, because
you are not here to hold
You are not here to embrace
me in your arms, or engulf
me in your love
I try to look for you in my
heart,
but all I have found are
empty spaces inert as ice
No warm, joy filled rooms
to welcome me...
just cold places with
nothing but empty spaces
There was no sunshine when
you left... you seized it all
You have taken my joy
with you... you are my
Joy
Please return, so that I may
smile once more

As I've So Stated

As I walk through the
    green grass,
  I think back to when I was
      loved
    Not that I'm not loved
        now,
    but I think back to when I could say
      I was in love too
    The grass seemed to be
      greener,
        and the roses were so much
        redder
I am intrigued by my constant
  happiness
  Not once did I worry about
    tomorrow,
    for tomorrow was another day of
  Love
But that joy is gone now
    Now, all I see is blue
    I guess that's why the
    sea seems so endless
      It seems so perfect!
    It is so blue, the
        sky accents its beauty
  Only the ocean loves now
    The great sea loves its
      inhabitants
    But as for me, I have no
      inhabitants
As I've so stated,
  I can only
    think back to when I was
      loved as I walk through the
    green grass

speaking of a gift

as i look at you picture and absorb
your beauty, i can only thank God for
sending such a blessing my way
your smile can brighten the
darkest day of my loneliest hour
the rays from your smile are so radiant,
they could supply the world light for ages
your smile is like the sun, but instead of heat,
it gives off love
your cheeks are like two stars
that glow in the tenebrous trials of life
your transcendental eyes could lure the most skilled
sailors off of their course
your lips are delectable delights that make the finest French
restaurants burn with envy
your hair is silky strands, that graciously
adorn your head
your satiny skin glows so that the world may
fall to its knees, and worship you
there is no greater gift, than you gracing
my life with your presence
if a man's desires could speak,
mine would be screaming your
name! no gift i give you could surpass the
gift you've given me
speaking of a gift, the gift that i have is
priceless among jewels and other
possessions one man may acquire
speaking of a gift, please adorn my heart with
your love...
i could love you a thousand nights, and during the day
seek to delight your soul! oh, that i may
give my spirit some purpose... consolation by simply
being near you
i can think of no other gift, than that of having
you as my very own
nothing else could possibly bring me so much joy

Letter To My Love

Hey baby,
How are you?
I hope this letter finds you true
I was feeling "poetic"
I saw a thought run through my head,
so I said let me get it,
and put it down on paper instead

Anyway, I was sitting here
thinking about how much I love you
and how much I need you in my life...
And as I came to a beautiful conclusion...
I do not need this kind of stress and strife!

You said when you met me,
that you were waiting to exhale...
But since we have been together,
you aint been nothing but HELL

You always screaming, "If you love me..."
IF?
Let me tell you something
If you can't see it,
I guess it wasn't meant for you to see
If I can not show you,
I damn sure can't tell you!
If you can not see it,
maybe I need to leave

If you didn't want a REAL lover
and all you wanted was a puppet,
you should have looked for Kermit

or some other Muppet
After being hurt as much as I have,
your emotions become numb
And after being with you,
it seems I have become dumb
See with me, there are no strings attached,
but it seems like you forgot that
If you think I was not there for you,
you must have lost your
mind
After all the defending and fighting
I did with my kin... you must
be blind

How do I love thee
let me count the ways...
Oh fuck it...
With you,
everything is a
simple ass phrase
I don't know what more
I can say
and
I don't know what more
I can do,
but if you think
I am going to stay with your
trifling tail...
listen to this...
WE ARE THROUGH!

So, take this how you
want to
And in the future, I hope your
madness cease
But I don't have a damn thing
left to say, except
PEACE

So You Thought

A child's days in this world
are numbered, and I must be
down for the count
That's how I
feel,
since my love has gone
Like a thief,
you came into my
life,
and stole everything I had
All I have left is
an ounce of
good health
and
a few dreams
Some dreams...
When you left,
you took many of
my dreams
and
inspirations
with you
Some health...
My body continues to
ache,
and
my heart
is broken
beyond repair
But somehow,
someway,
I'll make it
It will take some time,

but I know I'll be fine
You smothered the fire
we once had, and
you speak of
rekindling
the old flame!
But you,
of **all** people,
ought to know
you can't restart
what is over...
you start
ALL OVER AGAIN

So, while you are away,
I hope you find
what you need
But if you seek
love elsewhere,
here is a little advise...

When you think you found a better love,
you didn't
When you feel you've got a better love,
you don't
And when you think a better love wants you,
it won't
The grass may look better on the other side,
but it has just been fertilized
with more **shit**!
So you thought it was nice to take sometime
alone, well... enjoy

The Horizon

Let's meet on the horizon of a dream
A dream with
Purple skies and blue mountains
green seas and yellow trees
Let's mix up the color of everything,
so we can hide in the beauty of imagination
This is our world,
and it can be as jazzy as we want it to be
So,
Let's meet on the horizon of a dream
A dream with
Passion as our appetizer
and
Ecstasy as our entree
Let's make desire our destination,
and promise me we will never leave
This is our world,
and it can be as pleasing as we want it to be
So,
Let's meet on the horizon of a dream
A dream with
a meaningful me
and
a purposeful you
Let's define our destiny,
so we can support each other
This is our world,
and it can be as majestic as we want it to be
So,
Let's meet on the horizon of a dream
The horizon beckons
and
Life awaits

Satisfied

Nikki's Piece

You are my first thoughts in the morning,
and you are my last breathes at night
There is no pleasure in the sunrise
nor is there any comfort in a sunset,
without the joy of first knowing you
You encompass my every action,
making love an instant reaction
There is a certain peace
placed on my heart,
everytime I see you smile
To know beauty like yours,
I can only say I've been blessed
From the Mountains of Olympus
to the Waters of the Nile,
you have shown me beauty I
have only imagined
My pleasure is found in
you being satisfied
To not only know but feel love
in return is what I have
always searched for
I can truly say that
I have found my hearts desire
I am destined to love you,
as you are determined to embrace me

Strawberry Fields

Timing
Preparation
Placement
Covering every detail
prior to your arrival
Arrangements are already made...
Our alibi has
already been submitted
The phone will not be ringing
The door will not be knocked
For tonight, we shall
engage in your delight

Continue to creep in
cognizant of your coverings
I hope you left your
worries on the porch...
Now, leave your
dress by the door...
I want to relish the site
of candle flames against your skin
Even in darkness,
you are doubtlessly delicious
(This is seduction... don't be fooled)

The incense is already lit
The water is already drawn

The mood is already set
All you need to do is
submerge yourself
Close your eyes
Take a deep breath...
exchange your past problems,
for your present pleasures

I want to begin by
purifying your body, and
liberating your mind
As I relieve your body of the
sweaty salt I have been craving,
do you feel emancipated yet?
Has the scent settled in?
I like to prepare my prey
and you appear to be ready
Now as we let the stains
down the drain,
moistly proceed to the bed
Now is not the time to be dry
(This is seduction... don't be fooled)

The outstretched towel on the bed
is where you are to lay
Lie down on your belly...
this could not be complete without
me soothing your stressed muscles
(my fingers are not alone)
Let me light another incense...
Let me grab the feathers...
Let me get the oil...
Knowing how much I love the taste of
strawberries, is it any wonder why
I wish to cover you with them?
Strawberries suit you
If you do not yet know, I wish to

play in your strawberry fields
And when I am done, do you mind
if I get a drink from your wishing well?
I brought my own bucket
You said there was enough
for me to drink,
and when the heat of this rapture
exhausts me I will be thirsty
There...
Close your eyes
Count to ten
Make a wish
(This is seduction... don't be fooled)

Can you see it?
Can you smell it?
Can you taste it?
Can you feel it?
Illuming yet
Envisioned
Offensive yet
Obsessive
Unpalatable yet
Dainty
Disunioned yet
Scandalous
This is seduction... don't be fooled

For the next few hours,
I want you to sit
back, relax
and enjoy the ride
We have all night to
savor each other
Can you withstand the cold?
Are you ready for the
ice cream?

If you scream, I'll scream
We'll both scream
when I mix this cream
with your strawberries
I have no need for a spoon,
my tongue will suffice
"Anything's acceptable... just ask me,
and I'll try"
Tonight, there are no restraints
I only reserve the right
to order utter gratification
Tonight, we shall
engage in your delight and
I feel a blissful binge
coming on
Allow me the pleasure
of indulgence
I made this mess,
now let me lick this mess up

Uhn

The heat from your body
creates small trails of sweet enchantment
showing me the way
to your satisfaction
When I veer off the path,
another trail appears and reveals to me
the pending path to your pleasing
Am I there yet?
Are you coming with me?
If I left you behind,
I need to know...
This journey is not for me,
but it is for me to take you there

Ahh

There you are...
Squirming...
Clutching...
Shivering...
I see you came on
You want to take the lead?
By all means, be my guest...
If you know the way,
(and I am sure you do)
I would be more than ecstatic
to let you show me the light
Remember, tonight
we shall engage in
your delight
If you want me to come,
just tell me so
But please be gentle
I know where I
want to be, but if there
are other places you wish for me to go
then take me there

I am yours, and this
escapade is of your design

So, lead the way
Strawberries have never
been so damn sweet
As I approach the point
you wish for me to be,
I cannot help but wonder
if you want me to share what
I have found inside of me
This find could have been
discovered by anyone,
but it would never be so strongly felt

Uhn

You want to know what
it is that I know
Well now,
how shall this be shared?
I have been to the mountain top,
and now I know what it is to be known
I have seen the stars in Heaven,
and now I know why they dance
I have been to ecstasy,
and now I know I shall return...
tonight

You have shown me the
pleasures of a lifetime,
and I have embraced them
with a supreme satisfaction
The feelings you have invoked
cannot be counterfeited, imitated, or
fabricated
This is genuine
This is seduction... I have been fooled
It appears as though
I have been mislead
In my seduction,
I have been seduced
I have been taken
Take me there again
and I shall show you pleasures...
the same
This should never cease... no
We have done to much,
and seen so much,
that it would be a shame to never return
to the fields of our fancy

MOR

Death

ARS LONGA, VITA BREVIS - SENECA

Art is long, life is short

"Lots of people look at death as if it's a real villain.
I have come to the point, happily, where I've made peace with death...
Don't wait until tomorrow to tell somebody you love them.

Do it now" - Leo Buscalia

Vacant Tomb

Empty headstones and used dirt
supply the setting for my
transfiguration
Death, be not proud to serve my sentence
Whatever the ruling,
i am deserving
Whatever the judgment,
i have warranted
Whatever the condemnation,
i shall embrace commendably
i cannot speak against those
who have laid the foundation
for my fall, but i can
extend my gratitude
Profusely, i say, peace be your path
Though there were many
to plot and scheme my demise,
from the depths of the darkness yet i
rise

Laying In Wait

Have I been forsaken,
have I been overlooked?
　　But the Just One has made it
　　known to me that I'm to
　　　sow what I've reaped
For I have reaped that
　　that no man can stand
For I have reaped
　　loneliness

I have planted seeds of solitaire,
　　and now I must be a solitary child
I have looked up to the hills,
　　and no light has caught my eye
I have looked up to the hills,
　　and no dove has seen me
　　　Instead, I have looked up to the hills
　　and I have seen the clouds...
　　and the clouds have sent the rain
　　　to meet my eye in the sky
As I looked up to the sky,
　　the rain continued to fall on
　　　my soaking head

I felt like a tree, swaying
　　back and forth, looking
　　　for the sun...
　　but I found

no one
I can't stand the wind,
  cause it seems to knock
    me down all the time
      Like a tree with no roots,
I seem to topple to the
  ground

      Oh Gabriel, friend of mine, come!
    For this is all I ask,
      but even the Angels have forsaken me
I have cried and Azriel has
  heard me not!
    Have I been left here to lay
      in wait,
        or will there be one
    who will pity my groan?

Moon Over Me

I'm a prisoner in a world
I created
My problems are as thin string
attached to me, an oversized elephant
not knowing I could escape whenever I
please
I've been conditioned from birth
by the world to treat my
fears larger than
me
For shadows of the night
haunt me
The darkness of the day
The moon shines on all
that is, or
will ever be
From the moon, not the sun,
I draw my strength
For the moon shines on
all, and refrains on
none
The heat of the day is
content to accept the
protruding sun
But, the cool of the night
embraces the touch of the
moon
And one day, I shall

draw closer to my
strength
I shall pass all that
is, and the edge of all
will be behind me
Until then, I will absorb
my strength, and live
off of the light
Off of the night

Sky's Light

Tragedy seems to have found
  me at an unwelcome
    time
      It is like picking up the
    pieces of a broken glass
      You always get cut
    No matter how hard you try,
      a pretty piece finds its way home
        in your hand
      Do I deserve such pain?
      Am I feeling for purpose?
      Do I deserve this strain?
        Whether I deserve this end,
                    feel for reason,
                    or strain for cause...

      in my mind,
        I never feel the path
        I grace
        I only keep the leftovers
        I taste
      A tragic end, to
      A tragic beginning
        Not asked,
        Never received
Ill conceived is the
    notion, that some drink or
    potion will calm my body or mind
  Let me be that that I am...
the lonely man on the
    corner, waiting for a ride
  in the Sky's Light

I am the
        bastard child of
    Pride and Deception
        The ruler of none
                and
        The keeper of many
                Have I alms to bear?
                Am I bare in my alms?
    Barren and naked,
        this facade is
            dimming slowly
        like a candle in the wind
    Murmuring and bitter,
I beg for my end
    My pleas are plagued and
    my defense is distraught
    My muse is dead,
                        buried...
                            rising no more

        Clouds and shade
            depart from me,
        leaving me exposed to the
                tears of the stars
Do I weep as well?
    I feel my weeping
        ceased, when my heart
            sighed in the Sky's Light

All About Gain

If the saying is true...
If the saying is true that
to live is Christ and
to die is gain,
then is it wrong
to wish to die?
Is it a sin
to plan your own
death?
Like a story book that reads
perfectly,
Is it so bad
to gain?
Is it wrong
to want more?
Each day one strives
to get more, and everyday one seeks
to gain
Always wanting more,
but never getting enough
If the saying is true...
If the saying is true
to live is Christ and
to die is gain,
then is it wrong to truly wish to die?

Had It Not Been For Death

Why is it so hard to live after death?
Is it because we have come and gone,
Or has reality kicked in?
  Starting out, Death seemed so dreadful,
And appeared to be my enemy
My last ambition would have been
To talk with Death
When I was a child, I dreaded Death,
Dying, and everything associated with
Her
  But as I grew older, I began to
Understand
  That Death was only trying
To be my friend
                        Death was
Only trying to introduce Herself
To me
  As I talked with Death, She
Began to reveal Herself to me
  But it only took one stroll
For me to understand
                        Death
Was to be my comforter and
Ease the pain that life had given me
  So, had it not been for Death,
                  There would be no delight

Dead Leaves

It can't be Fall...
That's what I tell myself
It can't be Fall...
A Summer breeze blows over my head,
and I know it's not far away
Too many nights I have been thinking my end was near,
now I know time is up
But when you remember me,
don't leave no damn dead leaves
Yes we had problems... Yes we had issues...
Yes we had those things people say break up happy homes
But when you close your eyes,
do you really remember those things?
Do you delight,
or do you despair?
Do you think of the glory,
or do you think of the gloom?
Do you really waste time on things you wanted to change,
or do you think of things we changed?
Why concern yourself with matters you put aside,
and concern yourself with matters before you
Life is too wonderful to waste on yesterday...
Life is too short to worry about what didn't happen...
Life is too precious to pile dead leaves on...
As the Summer breeze blows,
the tree is relieved from the memory of what was
and works on what will be
The sadness departed decorations represent,
is no longer an issue
It is an after thought... a memory... history
So,
when you remember me,
don't leave no damn dead leaves

Purgatory

I'm wishing myself away
in my sorrows and my fears
Drowning in my depression
and
Dissolving in my Distress

Although Depression and Despair
are often beneficial,
this is not one of those times

I'm looking for my stairway now
Heaven can't be too far off
I know I'm early,
but I'm pressing for both
time and happiness

(Death has a way of making endings ironically sweet)

My mind has been open to
treason for some time now,
and my wounded spirit has no
solution for the anarchy that is in motion

Beware of the stranger dressed in
white linen
She has no remainder to offer

Rip my flesh from the bones,
and note that pain has not settled in
Pain only comes when there is
no alternative
From where I stand,
is there an alternative?

Love abandoned me tears ago
Compassion is nowhere to be found
and
Faith is too far off

I have no aid
I have no hope
I have no strength
I have nothing

AVE ATQUEVALE - CATULLAS
Hail and farewell

Acknowledgements

First and foremost, I want to thank GOD for making **all** these experiences and feelings possible. I have come to truly understand "He will **never** leave you, nor will he **forsake** you". Thank you Yah Veh Elohim!!!

To those who have shown me what love is and how to use it... thank you! You have made living a joy, as well as a pleasure. The **Amore** section would NOT be possible without those lessons. Kathie, thank you for giving me **a reason to love**! Loving you makes me remember the excuse to why I live.

Dr. T. F. Freeman and the TSU Debate Team, I love you all for the love you have shown me; Dr. J. Ward, Ms. Kelly and the **entire** Communications Department (present and past), thank you for the **life** lessons. Reuben Joseph, Mrs. Wilson and the print production team... **thank you** for teaching me about the process... **ALOT**!!! To the TSU family, thank you for your assistance, support, and love you have presented. I will **always** hold you dear to my heart.

Thank You's

Barbara "Gussie" Bogan, Sam, Lisa, and my Godson Rocky, Eric "E" and the entire Hunter Family, Desmond G. Moody, Herb "Mr. BNI", Victor "Stubby" Stubblefield, the East Sunnyside Court Subdivision residents, Anthony "International Lover" Frazier, Toni "Ms. New Power" Green... Ok, you know what? There are too many people I could send a thank you to, so, if I need to and I didn't send you a shout, **refer to the dedication**!!!!!

www.ingramcontent.com/pod-product-compliance
Lightning Source LLC
Chambersburg PA
CBHW071501070426
42452CB00041B/2033